PARABLES UP
THE MOUNTAIN

A SEEKER'S TRAIL

SkyRoot
Books

First edition
First print: April 2026
Printed on acid-free paper
ISBN: 979-8-9853522-2-1
Distributed by Ingram Content Group, Inc.

PARABLES UP THE MOUNTAIN

A SEEKER'S TRAIL

Joey Doherty

SkyRoot
Books

"Reading *Parables Up the Mountain* feels like walking beside someone who helps you slow down and breathe again. The pages become a mirror for your own inner path. A reminder that sacredness lives in the ordinary, and that nature still speaks if we're willing to listen."
– Iris Nabalo, Author of *Elemental Whispers*

"Every step feels like a heartfelt conversation with God, resonating deeply with the reader's own doubts, hopes, and yearnings. A journey that combines self-discovery with divine wisdom. This is not just a story—it's an invitation to reflect, to question, and to grow."
– Dhanya Varughese, Founder of Project Bluebird

"*Parables Up the Mountain* is the kind of book that reads you. It gives voice to the unique and shared experience of all honest seekers who come to discover that life itself is the curriculum. This book invites us to live from our spiritual heart, not with rigid prescriptions, but with courage, honesty, and compassion. You can read it in a single sitting or over a lifetime."
– Tyler D. Hudson, PhD, Psychotherapist & Professor

"Spiritual and religious concepts intertwine in a harmonious tapestry of wisdom. A lyrical invitation to find peace amidst the FAQ's of life. A loving embrace of our perfectly imperfect humanity. As someone healing from religious trauma, this book helped me reframe what I found harmful in religious dogma. I'll reread at hard moments, for a reminder that it's all much simpler than we often make it."
– Kelly Kohlberg, Artist & Educator

CONTENTS

"If a man wishes to be sure of the road he treads
on, he must close his eyes and walk in the dark."

- St. John of the Cross

A BEGINNING

I toss my phone into the rusty trash can at the trailhead along the coast. The screen cracks against a jagged rock. There's no turning back now.

I take a shallow breath and start walking east, hopefully toward the master on the mountaintop. My backpack is full. My boots are broken in. I'm as ready as I'll ever be.

The yellow bird tells me the master accepts one student per lifetime and has yet to select his apprentice. I am determined to be that apprentice.

I take another step and feel the ocean breeze nudge me along. Almost as if the wind is blessing my pilgrimage. Nah, probably not, but I could use all the blessings I can get.

My life is in ruins, and I need direction. I need answers. I no longer fit into the world I built around myself. My career, my community, even my personality is up in the air. The truer me is rising to the surface, and the old me is putting up a fight.

Worst of all, I don't know who God is.

I have explored just about every spiritual and religious tradition I could get my hands on. One community feels exhilarating, but dangerous. Another feels safe, but rigid. The God of one circle is packed neatly into a box, and the God of another circle is nowhere to be found.

I am a man without a spiritual home.

I do wonder if there is some truth to Jesus, the real Jesus, but religion is not my thing. I crave an authentic path that's both freeing and grounded.

It's time to get away from the rushed opinions of society and rediscover myself in the wilderness. I suspect the master on the mountaintop has the answers I am seeking.

But first, I must find him.

The air smells less salty the further I walk from the coast. The sound of crashing waves now replaced with buzzing insects. They say the first step is the hardest, but I don't believe it. As lost as I am, I still feel lighter walking alone with this heavy backpack than I did all those years comfortably taking no steps at all.

One thing is certain—I'd rather be true and alone than false with others.

After rounding a muddy corner and praying like I did when I was young and on fire, I see a man leaning on a bent staff with a long goatee and gray hair bursting out of his hat. Only a small knapsack on his back. He appears to be daydreaming, looking out into nothing. I am annoyed. I want to take this pilgrimage on my own, so I can prepare myself for the master on the mountaintop.

I keep walking and the strange man looks my way with a nod of the head. He waits for me to get within earshot and says, "Hello, fellow wanderer! You can call me Coyote. It appears we are walking the same path. May I join you?"

Just as I am about to decline his offer, I notice a faded section of his poncho right over his chest. Actually, there is something oddly familiar about him. I feel held and puzzled at the same time.

Before I can think of a response, the words pour out as if pushed and pulled at the same time, "Sure, let's walk together. It's smart to travel with a companion out here."

Coyote responds, "Splendid, but I have one condition. From here on, I will only speak when asked a heartfelt question."

THE RAINFOREST

After walking several miles in silence, I ask, "What have you heard about the master on the mountaintop?"

Coyote responds, "There is no lecturing out here. No telling you how to live. Yet there are masters every direction you look."

I ask, "What do you mean?"

Coyote responds, "Open your eyes and you will see. Open your ears and you will hear. Open your heart and life will open right up to you."

He points with his staff, and continues, "Over there, trees displaying strength. Over here, rivers displaying consistency. And right under our feet, moss displaying collaboration and trust.

All around us are teachers with nothing to prove. Nothing to sell. Only an invitation, and you can take it or leave it. Those are the masters with something worth listening to."

I whisper to myself, "I am in for a wild journey if I continue walking with this strange man."

***

I ask, "Why are you alone in the wilderness?"

Coyote responds, "Oh, I am not alone when the hawk swoops down and the frogs chatter at night and the trees sway from an almost-deadly gust of wind.

I am not alone when the old footprints on the trail feel like my own and my cold hands embrace the breeze and the smile on my face sends fire to my limbs.

I am not alone when the crickets remind me that music is everywhere, if I listen. And I remember that I am also part of the symphony. My breath a wind instrument. My fingers a string instrument when reaching out to the tall grass. My eyes a subtle meditation bell that rings everywhere I toss a heavy gaze.

You ask why I am out here in the wilderness. Well, this. More and more of this."

I nod, as if I understand. It's becoming clear that Coyote won't give me straight answers, which is annoying. Yet, I can't help but crave more of his words. I have a long journey ahead and might as well be entertained.

✳✳✳

I notice a squirrel fall from a branch. Luckily, it lands on its feet and runs off. I ask, "Does nature make mistakes?"

Coyote smiles, "First of all, do not take anything I say as fact. Filter my words through the veins of experience, in and out of your heart-shaped compass.

The wisdom you seek is not found in words, but we shall play around with words for now.

As for your question, whether nature makes mistakes depends on how narrow the window is that you're looking through. It depends how willing you are to be surprised, to be proven wrong, to adjust the tight strap on your hat and release this need to know how the world works. It depends how well you can live for a moment in another's shoes."

I say, "I don't understand."

Coyote continues, "From our isolated human perspective, when a squirrel falls from a branch and hits the ground, we see this as a mistake. However, to the squirrel, maybe it was the ride of his life because he finally got to fly for a few wild moments!

Maybe the squirrel did make a mistake, but God watched the whole thing like a film director who still gets choked up watching His early films.

Maybe the squirrel's fall taught his brothers and sisters a valuable lesson—be careful when chasing those flower-loving birds that buzz so loud you get mesmerized and find yourself in between a waking and sleeping dream that doesn't end with unlimited acorns but with a headache that's only relieved by forgiving that innocent hummingbird.

Perhaps whether it is a mistake depends on the squirrel getting up and learning. Perhaps whether it is a mistake depends on someone, somewhere learning. Perhaps whether it is a mistake depends on nothing at all, because whether we hold our faith out in the open or hidden in our pocket, God is there and the natural world bends at His will."

I take time to think while we continue walking. Coyote's words are peculiar. On one hand, I understand what he's saying, and on the other, I have no clue whatsoever.

✳✳✳

I ask, "What is your work? Did you ever feel unsure of your path?"

Coyote responds, "My work is not important at this time, but I expect it is familiar to you. And yes, I felt unsure many times. Faith is not an absence of doubt, my friend. In fact, true faith requires moments of uncertainty. If you never question the path, then your steps aren't really your own."

Coyote kneels down to pick up a broken stick, and continues, "Perhaps we are all walking around a little lost and in a childlike way seeking directions. We ask one another, 'Where is God? Where can I find love? When did you last see them?' And the Good Shepherd places holy breadcrumbs in our path in the form of teachers who provide the best directions they can, based on their own world."

I ask, "How did you find your way?"

Coyote responds, "I took the third left next to the Big Tree, and then a giant boulder fell from the cliff and forced me to go another way, which is exactly where I needed to go, where I found what I wasn't looking for."

***

Coyote leaps from boulder to boulder like a mountain goat who knows this trail better than anyone. He even has the wispy goatee. I've never seen someone who walks with a staff move with such speed. Such grace. He appears both old and young at the same time.

I shout, "How do you move so effortlessly? You're like a goat!"

Coyote laughs, "I travel light!"

I catch up with him and say, "But how do you survive out here carrying such a small knapsack? Don't you worry you will run out of food and water?"

He responds, "Tell me, where did you get your backpack?"

I say, "I bought it in a small, cobblestone mountain town from a man who made it by hand. He didn't speak my language, but I trusted his work."

Coyote responds, "Interesting. Now, who knows what the pack can hold, you or the maker?"

I say, "The maker, of course."

Coyote replies, "Yes, the maker knows what the pack can hold and what it is not meant to hold by its design. And this is how it is with the Maker of the Universe. He knows what you can handle and what you need to trust in His care, because He designed you.

So as for me, I only carry what is mine to carry and offer the rest to my Maker, who can handle whatever I toss His way."

I nod, remove my backpack, and see that it is bulging at the seams.

$$***$$

Coyote walks toward a large boulder shaped differently than the others, and I follow. I hear bubbling that grows stronger and stronger until eventually, I see water flowing from a crack in the stone, forming a small brook.

Directly above the crack are three lines carved into the stone. The symbol looks old. Very old.

Coyote squats like a frog, rubs his chest while silently speaking what seems like a prayer, and lets the water pour into his mouth.

I quickly ask, "Is this water safe to drink?"

Coyote smirks, "Has fear ever quenched your thirst? I tell you, the first time I tasted this spring, which has now nourished me for decades, I wondered why I had been drinking stale water from a faucet my entire life. And still, this spring does not compare to the Living Spring that quenches the soul."

I walk towards the flowing water and look at Coyote to decide if I trust this stranger who leaps from boulders and speaks in riddles. As I examine him, a yellow bird glides over his head. He doesn't

even flinch. It's like he and the bird have an understanding.

Coyote tosses a nod of reassurance my way, and
I cup my hands to catch some water. It's crystal clear.
Colder than I expected, which is refreshing on a hot
afternoon. I notice my reflection in the water, then
take a sip with eyes closed.

***

I say, "You have mentioned God a few times. Do you think we can ever fully understand the divine?"

Coyote responds, "God does not ask to be fully understood. He asks to be communed with. To be known on an intimate level. To be trusted without understanding His every move."

I say, "But how can I trust a God whose image is cloudy to me?"

Coyote looks up at the sky, and says, "Attempting to capture God is like capturing a photo of the moon. We can try, but let's remember that the photo is still a photo. It will never be the real thing.

Better to grab a hand and soak up that illuminating presence. Then you will see if there truly is a face on the moon or perhaps something even more familiar, something beyond comprehension, something deeper than we can capture with words."

I say, "I hear you, but I still want to figure out who God is. Humor me. Who is God to you?"

Coyote replies, "God is in the space between my inhale and exhale. God is in my hand as I turn suffering into art. God appears in fullness here and in pieces out there. Three strands woven into One, connecting us all. The One between all things. The One weaving the bee to the flower. The One weaving you to me. The One encompassing all. God is our greatest potential, served up on a never-ending platter and thankfully, we get to be hungry. We get to climb high or dive low or fumble our way through life, and still, we get to meet God through a simple moment. God allows an ocean to wave and a tree to flower and a human to die. God is eternal life through an innocent death. God is in my heart, and I am in the heart of God."

I whisper to myself, "Fascinating, but that didn't clear things up at all."

Then I say out loud, "What God do you follow?"

Coyote responds, "I follow Christ. I follow Him to the ends of the earth and further still. He is my compass, and I aim to walk more like Him every day."

I pause, then say, "Aren't you going to try to convert me?"

Coyote laughs, "No, but I will walk with you."

I nod, and make a mental note to circle back to this topic.

Coyote says we cannot fully capture God, yet he follows a specific path to God, through Christ. It doesn't make sense. Still, I appreciate him not forcing his beliefs onto me. He is not like any Christian I've met, that's for sure.

$$***$$

We pass what looks like a crumbling statue of a man covered in moss. I look to Coyote and say, "I feel close to discovering my purpose, but also far away. You seem so sure of yourself. What has helped you?"

Coyote responds, "It's not about discovering anything. It's about unlearning what is keeping you from hearing God's voice. Just as a sculptor carefully removes marble from the statue, God asks you to remove the pieces of clay and mud and even marble you have picked up over your lifetime that are distracting you from His masterpiece.

This is a co-creation. Remember that. You cannot create a life without Him, and He also needs you to reach out and grab His hand, like a child to his spiritual Father.

Consistently check in with yourself along the way to be sure that you are sculpting a statue of you, the real you, God's image of you, rather than the world's image of you. And when you make a mistake and regret breaking off a piece of your statue, remember that these days are just as necessary as the days with steady hands."

****

I ask, "What does it mean to be holy?"

Coyote responds, "It's not that one thing carries a piece of the divine and another does not. It's all holy! We simply cannot see it at times. We look for a thing, but it's the connection between things that is holy. It's the relationship, and lucky for us, our relations are endless."

I ask, "What do you mean?"

Coyote continues, "There is no separation between the Colombian butterfly and the drought-ending Mexican rain. There is no separation between that unspoken dream and your sore throat. There is no separation between Yeshua's many prayers in the desert and your moment of clarity while praying like a child after years of wounded silence. There is no separation between the struggles of our cave-dwelling ancestors and our busy unwillingness to enter the cave of our own shadows.

The holiness lies in our willingness to do our part, and trust is the key that gets us through that door of connection. Our inability to see beauty in a wilting flower does not mean the flower is ugly. The problem lies within us, and this inability to witness beauty momentarily severs one of those holy threads.

But take heart, because the thread is never completely severed. Remember that. It's up to us all to reach out our hands, time and time again, rejoining the holy tapestry."

I ask, "How do we live in harmony with the world?"

Coyote responds, "Get intimate with the world around you. The trees love to feel your gaze. The tall grass loves to feel your touch. The shallow river loves to feel you tiptoe through its rock-filled waters. The stars love to be witnessed from afar.

Allow your breath and the wind to dance with each other, in and out, until they become more similar than different. See more overlap between the wind and your breath, and you will see just how similar we all are at our core."

I stop walking and try to listen to my breath. Then to the wind. Then to my breath again.

I'm not sure what I should be listening for, but whatever it is, I don't hear it. I don't have time for this, anyway, so I get back to walking, hopefully toward the master on the mountaintop.

***

I ask, "Do you think we have free will or that God has it all planned out?"

Coyote responds, "This is one of those topics that our human intellect cannot comprehend, but I suspect both are true."

I ask, "How can both be true?"

Coyote says, "Tell me, how do you make sure you continue breathing while you sleep?"

I respond, "Well, I don't. It just happens."

Coyote responds, "Yes, much of your breathing happens unconsciously, behind the scenes. And still, you can consciously slow your breathing when you need to relax. Both are true."

"I don't understand," I say.

Coyote responds, "Look at the farmer. Certain tasks are his responsibility. Planting the seeds. Watering the soil. Connecting previous generations with the current generation by composting scraps into the dirt.

The farmer has his duties, and carrying them out increases the chances that the farm flourishes. Yet he cannot make the sun shine. He cannot make the rain pour. He cannot force a seed to turn into a great orchard. Those alone are God's duties.

God cannot plant the seeds for you, and you cannot control the harvest. Tend to your soil and trust God to provide the sun and rain."

***

A strong gust of wind blows, and I ask, "How can I learn to see where God is guiding me?"

Coyote asks, "Can you see the wind?"

I say, "No, I cannot. But I see what the wind touches."

"Exactly," he says. "There is more wisdom within you than you realize. The wind is invisible to your rational eyes that want desperately to understand what is happening. But you can see what the wind touches. The trace it leaves. The gentle and curious woosh pulling the hawk where he needs to go next."

We take a moment to listen and watch the trees swaying back and forth. Then the wind settles, and out of nowhere, a hawk glides over the horizon of treetops. It seems to be heading toward a clearing in the trees.

Coyote and I look at each other, nod, and follow the hawk.

THE CANYON

We made it through the rainforest. This Coyote guy is peculiar. Yet, I trust him for some reason. He seems like a good man.

Anyway, I have so many questions. I don't know where I belong or what I'm meant to do in this life. What I do know is I feel suffocated in most churches and uneasy in new age circles. One community feels too closed off and the other feels too open. Each has what the other lacks. It seems so obvious, but how to move forward?

I need an example of an authentic merging of the spiritual and religious. I don't want to lose the depth or the mystery. But is it possible to be mystical while remaining grounded? I don't want to water down Christ's true teachings. But is it possible to have a relationship with Christ that's authentic and freeing?

Perhaps the master on the mountaintop can help. Hopefully Coyote isn't too much of a distraction.

****

We sit on the edge of a cliff, and I ask, "What is the secret to life?"

Coyote bursts out laughing for much longer than I'd prefer, then finally says, "Okay, find a tree that grabs your attention, down on the other side of the canyon. Then stare at the tree, breathing into it as much as it is breathing into you."

I glare at Coyote, and realize he is serious. I have no idea how to breathe into a tree. Then again, this man seems to know a few things and I'm desperate, so I give it a shot.

I search the canyon and find an interesting tree. After several restless minutes of trying to force something enlightening to happen, I begin to settle into my breath and the tree. Deeper and deeper. I'm not sure what is happening, but it's incredible.

Some time goes by, and Coyote says, "Tell me what you experienced."

I say, "Well, I'm questioning what I saw, but I think the tree turned into the whole forest for a moment. Sort of a never-ending ecosystem not bound by trees but including all life. The waterfall, the hawks flying above, the fish accidentally jumping from the top of that chaotic falling water down to the serene swimming hole. It was beautiful."

Coyote nods, "Become as steady and true as the hawk's beating heart as he dives to honorably kill his prey, and you will see the threads weaving it all together. You don't need a secret key. Everything is already unlocked, and a present, willing heart gets you in that sacred door."

$$*\,*\,*$$

I nervously say, "I see beauty in these trees and all of the natural world, but I struggle to see beauty in myself. How can I show myself the same acceptance?"

Coyote looks into my eyes with great care, and says, "Even if the rain were to forget that sometimes it takes the shape of river, sometimes ocean, sometimes blood flowing through a human's veins, the connection is still there. The resemblance is still there. And despite your forgetting, God's image is carved into your heart, one breath away."

I say, "I wish I believed that."

Coyote responds, "I want you to close your eyes. Imagine a child running towards you. Suddenly, he trips and scrapes his knee."

I visualize this scene, and instantly feel immense love for that unknown, hurting child.

And Coyote says, "The same way you look at a child when your wonder bleeds into love is how God looks at you when you do anything at all."

****

I say, "There are moments when I feel God's love. Then it's gone. Why does God keep me waiting?"

Coyote responds, "It is all an in-between season. Never perfectly winter or perfectly spring or perfectly summer or autumn.

The shades of brown in the muddy river are endless, and so are the shades of love. How could it be any other way?

One morning, the family of deer runs playfully through your yard, and the next evening the spotted one is stuck in the river crying for help from anyone who cares to listen, no matter if you walk on four legs or two, and you get to decide if it's better to step in or let nature run its course.

Seasons within seasons. Choices within choices.

The river rising and falling as ancestor rain brings what the river doesn't know it needs. A river wears winter nicely. And spring. And summer. And the blushing season.

The tall grass gets weighed down by the rising stream and then perks up with the sun, and back and forth she goes, never on schedule but always on time.

All these twists and turns in the river, and you thought the fish were swimming towards one destination, but they've been dancing with the current this whole time. Free of the battle between good or bad, this season or that season."

***

I say, "I am trying to be patient, but I want out of this season of life. What if it doesn't end?"

Coyote responds, "While listening to a favorite song, do you skip to the chorus and shove off the rest like it's an unfortunate detour?"

I respond, "Well, no."

Coyote continues, "Then why do you treat your life this way? You are trying to play God by forcing yourself out of a season of healing in order to sing the chorus once again. It doesn't work that way.

You've forgotten that you can sing the whole way through! A melody works because it's the highs and the lows, the light and the dark, the pain and the peace.

You know this already. You have for some time, and the forgetting is as much a part of the song as the remembering."

***

I step over a fallen tree and the loose rocks shift under my feet, causing me to stumble. After checking my knee and seeing blood on my fingers, I look up at Coyote and say, "I can handle physical pain, but it's pain of the heart that knocks me down and keeps me down."

A tear tries to surface, but I stuff it inside and say, "Coyote, how can I heal from heartbreak?"

He sits next to me on the dusty ground and places his right hand on my left shoulder. After several moments of silence, he says, "Your pain is real, my friend. I will not take it away, but I will walk with you as long as it takes. May I pray?"

"Yes," I surprisingly say. And I immediately feel a mysterious peace.

Coyote removes his shoes and prays, "Master Healer, I invite you here with us. Thank you for bringing us pilgrims together. Thank you for your light above and your roots below. I ask that you soften our hearts, so we can receive your healing touch. I ask that you open our ears, so we can hear your voice. I ask that you continue revealing yourself to us. In Christ's name I pray, Amen."

I say, "I appreciate your prayer, but I still want to know how to heal from heartbreak."

Coyote responds, "The Master Healer is in everything, although He is more accessible in living things. And few things are more alive than pain."

"I don't understand," I say, now frustrated.

Coyote continues, "Look at your wound. Red-hot concentrated life is rushing to your knee. Your body's loving instinct, nursing you like a mother does a crying baby.

And with pain of the heart, it is not blood that rushes in, but the Healer Himself. The problem is that much of the time, we do not welcome His tender care. We move through suffering with hands clenched, stubbornly closed off to miracles. Closed off to the wisdom of grief.

We forget that God cherishes the brokenhearted. He loves everyone, but prioritizes the brokenhearted because they need Him most. But He will never force Himself. It's our decision to receive His support or not.

And so, there are few things in this world more important than suffering, because suffering brings us closer to God, if we allow it."

$$***$$

I say, "I listen to your words and resonate, or read a quote and feel inspired, but then I go on with my day. How do I integrate what I learn into everyday life?"

Coyote responds, "Presence. God also lives in the mundane. The problem is that most of us are not yet masters of presence, so we do not experience Him there. It takes a great deal of practice to see the sacred in the mundane.

To the untrained mind, church is required to feel God's presence. Intensity is required to feel something. Prayer with hands folded and knees bent. Great epiphanies with veils lifted and curtains torn.

These are wonderful moments, yet to the trained mind, even the crickets at night can be a prayer. Even the first sip of coffee, the clock ticking, the cracks in the sidewalk as you walk to the same bus day after day.

God is always ready to meet you where you are. You do not need to be a saint to live in the Kingdom of Heaven, but you do need to be like a child.

If you want to follow God's plan, learn to remain present with Him without the spiritual highs or lows. If you depend on the lightning striking, you are not much use to His living plan. You have put your fleeting emotions in charge of your life instead of the One with infinite wisdom.

I see you are in a season of crumbling and rebuilding. Feel it and meet God there. Take the leap and meet God there. Follow your intuition even if others think you're crazy, and I assure you, God is there waiting to congratulate you. To give you a hug. To place His hand over your heart and remind you that He loves you. He formed that heart in your chest, and although His ways will not always make sense to you, they are for you. They are always for you."

I say, "Success arrives quickly for others, and here I am, spinning around in circles. What if I am on the wrong path?"

Coyote responds, "That is their path. This is yours. A true path is one of a kind. There is no guidebook. It must be lived, not planned."

I say, "I wish mine was an easier path."

Coyote responds, "Be wary of the pleasant path. The Good Shepherd does not operate this way. The deceiver disguises himself as an angel of light and offers treasures of this world for those who want a shortcut. This false angel places breadcrumbs in your path leading to your pride, while the Good Shepherd places breadcrumbs leading to your soul.

Some call these moments synchronicities. When people cross paths with you at the perfect time, or an opportunity presents itself when you need it most, ask yourself if this moment is guiding you towards God or further away. The posture of your heart shapes these moments.

Be discerning with those who ask for riches and swiftly receive riches. Who ask for fame and swiftly receive fame. Who want something for their own benefit, and it is swiftly given to them.

The wide path brings treasures on earth, while the narrow path brings everlasting life beyond imagination. Allow your way to unfold as you take each step, through faith."

I respond, half joking and half serious, "You aren't making it sound very appealing to follow God."

Coyote smiles, "One simple second in God's presence is greater than ten thousand lifetimes of getting everything you want."

Coyote then closes his eyes, rubs his chest, and silently speaks to himself.

I remain silent. This seems like a sacred moment.

Once he opens his eyes, I say, "May I ask why you rubbed your chest like that?"

Coyote replies, "I allowed my discernment to bleed into judgment, so I asked for forgiveness. Only God can see into the heart of man."

Coyote pulls out a hand drawn map, and I say, "I've never seen a map like this. Where did you get it?"

Coyote responds, "I come from a long line of map makers. My maps look different from those of my ancestors, but our goal is the same—to map the seen and unseen world.

Although I do not agree with some of my ancestors about the shape of the earth, there is still great wisdom in their old maps. They paved the way, same as those before them. We all come from somewhere, and there is truth deep down if you know how to look through the curious eyes of a child rather than the stubborn eyes of an adult."

I say, "Interesting, and not easy for me to do. I bet you have explored many beautiful places. You know, I would like to see a map of all the different names people use for God. There must be thousands! It's overwhelming."

Coyote responds, "Yes, there are places where many gods are worshipped instead of One. There are lands with names you cannot pronounce. There are even lands no man has set foot on yet. The world around you and the world within you dance back and forth. Remember that."

"What do you mean?" I ask.

Coyote replies, "If you were raised in a community that refers to God as 'Creator,' then creation is the lens you naturally see God through.

If you were raised in a region held captive by droughts, then your prayers are for rain, not sun.

If your homeland is known for its eternal blue sky, then your image of God may have a striking blue face unlike any other place on earth.

If your ancestors hunted caribou in a land where snow does not allow for long growing seasons, then the campfire stories filter through this cold, brutal way of life that makes way for faith in the straight arrow.

And if you were raised in a community that dares not give God a name and instead believes the sound of breath, whether in times of peace or times of struggle, is the closest sound we can muster up to describe God, then you may have little interest in capturing God and instead seek to simply be with Him.

Do you see? Your childhood, your land, your ancestors, your stories, it all shapes the divine in your mind's eye.

Now it is up to you to figure out which qualities from your lineage allow you to be closer to God and which qualities are getting in the way. Only you can uncover this. It was people and situations outside of you that planted these concepts inside of you, and now it's your job to sift through to see what is gold to you and what is gold to another.

A map is useful, but it only points to the real thing. Eventually, you must go and see for yourself, which you have begun. So learn from the maps you were given, then create your own, and then burn them all and toss the ashes into the soil, and see what grows in their place."

****

I say, "I know I am meant for more in this life, but I don't know what that is or how to get there."

Coyote responds, "It's not your job to have it all figured out. It's not your job to know your destination or to even know your next three steps. That is God's job.

You are here to be human. You are here to live. To love. To be of service. To try your best to follow His plan. To lean into truth. To take paths you aren't entirely certain of. To take a painful step. To flirt with insanity. To make mistakes and own up to them. To stumble and get back up."

I say, "You make it sound so simple, but it's complicated."

Coyote responds, "My friend, you do not need to act, speak, or think perfectly in order for God's plan to unfold perfectly.

The sacred path is not about perfection, but about living imperfectly with God in your heart."

✳✳✳

I say, "I want to be pure in thought and action. Do you think the master on the mountaintop can help me?"

Coyote responds, "It is said that the angels rejoice more over one broken sinner who has repented than ninety-nine, gold-covered holy men who seemingly have nothing to repent for.

It appears God and His warriors know something we forget—a saint is not born of roses. A saint is co-created between God and a man who takes more than a few unfortunate turns. Who tries with all his might to love, and sometimes this leads to accidentally harming others to avoid himself, then he repents and tries again. This is the saint.

The stronger the desire to please the Lord, the harder the fall when it doesn't go as planned. It's the risk-takers that please Him, not those playing it safe.

Better to be an honest rascal than a phony saint. It's the honest rascal that makes God weak in His knees."

✳✳✳

I ask, "What do you think happens after we die?"

Coyote responds, "I suspect that when you build an intimate relationship with the divine in this life, you then guide your kin from the afterlife. You make God more accessible to your kin, whether your blood runs through their veins or not. Let this motivate you."

I ask, "Motivate me to do what?"

Coyote responds, "To connect with all that is holy in this life. To grow into a golden leaf on one branch of the holy tree, so your kin can one day become a leaf on the branch of their choosing."

I ask, "How do I do that?"

Coyote responds, "Work towards the center every day. Tune in. Connect. It's not enough to speak about God. You must speak with Him."

✱✱✱

I say, "My feet have blisters, and my back is sore from carrying this heavy pack. What keeps you going?"

Coyote responds, "The spring wildflowers before they burst through the soil. Their presence is so natural you can feel them before you can see them, if you care to take off your shoes and listen in the old ways. This brings me back. What we have different imperfect words for. What brings a laugh and a tear at the same time."

Coyote looks my way, and says, "Tell me, what do you hear?"

I listen for a second, and say, "Nothing. I hear nothing."

Coyote responds, "Hmm. What does this nothing sound like?"

I listen again, this time with my ears and my feet, and say, "Well, I guess it sounds like thousands of whispering insects. Actually, not just insects, but the wind too, and the trees creaking while swaying in the wind."

Coyote responds, "Ah yes, a symphony. What a treat."

THE VALLEY

I admit, it's nice walking with Coyote. Sometimes we go miles without speaking. I appreciate that because I need lots of time to ponder.

Still, I don't know how much longer I can go. It feels as if I am relearning how to walk. I used to think God did not exist. Then I thought every god was true. And now, I'm not so sure.

I used to think I had all the answers. This way of thinking made me feel empowered for a while, but now it's lonely.

I am praying again, which is comforting, but I don't know where to direct my prayers. I don't know who to lean on when I have nowhere else to turn. So what's the solution? One God?

That's a big commitment, especially for someone who avoided the word 'God' for years. But it's difficult to relate to a God without a face. And my prayers to an ambiguous God have opened me up to spiritual things that feel unsafe.

Anyway, we'll see what tomorrow holds.

✳✳✳

We arrive at a crossroads, and I ask, "Which way leads to the master?"

Coyote responds, "What if you ask this river? Or the wind? Or the crumbled leaf in your hand? God has woven subtle messengers into creation, waiting patiently for you to ask the right question and be willing to receive a true answer."

I respond, "Okay, I'll play along."

Coyote smiles and says, "Tell me about the veins of the leaf in your hand."

I look at the leaf and say, "I see veins going this way and veins going that way, and I suppose they all reach the edge eventually. Okay, I think I understand. You're saying it doesn't matter which direction we go because we'll reach the master eventually?"

Coyote laughs, "Not me. The leaf is saying that!"

I accidentally let out a chuckle.

Coyote continues, "One direction will get you there smoothly, while the other will be a detour that shapes you into the man who is ready to meet the master."

***

We continue walking along the river, and I say, "This journey is taking much longer than I expected. I want to turn back, but what if I regret it?"

Coyote responds, "There is no rush. You will get where you need to go. It likely won't happen when or how you think it should.

There will be rocks in your stream, fallen logs, kayakers bursting around the corner to turn your peaceful evening into one with unannounced laughter and unforgettable change of plans.

Sometimes you'll float down on a green leaf, and sometimes you'll be what the leaf knows it can be.

Steady, says the river. Go steady.

You are always going somewhere, even when you try not to, so might as well go steady. Hold onto a branch if you lose your balance. Swim to shore if you forget how to breathe like a human.

A river will tell you, you are not a river, so stop trying to be one!

Flail your arms if you need to. It's only a race if you think it is. There is no enlightened point on the map, and all the rivers connect anyway.

Let the rain fill you up and the sun dry you out. Let the heart be your compass and let the mind tire itself running all around town."

***

I say, "You seem so joyful. What's the trick to creating a life of ease?"

Coyote replies, "I will share a story. There was a man who owned a mulberry orchard. For many years, his orchard provided the town with fruit for pies, jams, and wine.

One day, the man was annoyed of bugs eating the berries, so he sprayed the trees with chemicals. But the berries no longer tasted right.

He grew tired of watering and pruning, so he attached plastic leaves. But the shade those leaves provided no longer satisfied the birds.

Eventually, he convinced the mulberry trees that they were pines, and the saplings grew confused, dreaming of the seasons while carrying leaves that neither fall with the snow nor bud with the flowers.

Generations later, the man's granddaughter became inspired to bring the orchard back to its natural state. She removed the fake leaves. She tended the soil the hard way. She watered the trees daily and on those hot days with her own sweat.

Eventually, true leaves grew back, and birds returned for shade. The mulberries tasted better than ever, and bugs returned for food. But this time they ate the leaves, not the fruit. Instead of killing the bugs, she invited them to feed on certain trees.

Soon, she realized that these bugs were not ene-mies, but silkworms. The weavers of sacred fabric, right here in her orchard.

And so, a natural agreement was made. Once the silkworms emerged from their cocoon, the orchard produced white silk for those ready to receive a new name."

✳✳✳

I ask, "How do I let go of my mistakes?"

Coyote responds, "Look around you. Just as these rocky cliffs have cracks for animals to make a home, there are cracks within you for God to seep in and fill with a peace only He can provide.

But you must be open to receive Him. And He could come at any moment, so you must learn to remain open as often as you are able."

I ask, "How do I remain open?"

Coyote responds, "Empty yourself on the bare mud and roll around with a prayer in your heart. Then wash anew in the stream and see what part of yourself the mud sticks to.

This is the way of the saints, and we are all saints deep down. There is no man without a past, and the key is to love the mud with such clarity that it rises to the surface instead of hiding in your depths.

This is how you become free. Then you will see that a mistake ceases to be a mistake once you allow it to draw you closer to God."

***

I say, "My mind is all knotted up. I want one thing, and I'm not so sure that thing is actually good for me. It feels like seven people live inside my head, all at war with one another. How can I find clarity?"

Coyote asks, "What happens when you tug on a knot? When you try to force it free?"

I say, "It becomes more stuck. More tense. You make the knot worse."

Coyote responds, "Correct. This is how it is with your knotted mind. Clarity cannot be forced.

I see that you think a great deal, and this is admirable, but be mindful where you place all this care. You have flipped this passion on yourself, and this helps no one.

Place your passion where it is useful. Not towards fixing yourself or fixing anything at all, but towards a divine calling. Then, your spare time will no longer be spent forcing that energy into mental loops."

I interrupt, "I see what you are saying about loosening up. But how do I find a calling to devote my passion to?"

Coyote responds, "That is a conversation between you and God. And try to listen more than you speak. Try to see more than you think."

Before I could respond, Coyote suddenly walks off the trail. I naturally follow through the thick forest, but after a few steps he looks back and motions for me to stay where I am. I'm confused. Then I realize I've been asking questions for miles, and I'm sure he needs solo time, like me. He was out here alone in the wilderness when we met, after all.

I find a fallen tree, sit down, and look back at Coyote, who is now further away and mysteriously kneeling as still as a boulder at the base of a waterfall that I didn't notice until now. The water is a deep turquoise. It almost looks like a painting.

I give Coyote his space and try to listen to God with my eyes closed. Several minutes go by, and I hear nothing. Only more twisted up thoughts.

Before giving up, I consider speaking with Christ instead of this ambiguous God who is difficult to reach, and I immediately get distracted and open my eyes to a frog on the tree in front of me.

What a pleasant surprise. I haven't seen a tree frog in years. Bright green with that deep orange on his belly.

I remember the technique Coyote taught me at the canyon, and I breathe into the frog as much as he is breathing into me.

What a captivating creature, effortlessly sticking to the tree like those glue sticks I used as a child when making crafts at the dining table. A God who formed this creature must be wise, and wildly crea-tive.

I feel my body loosening up, and I fall into a much-needed sleep.

✳✳✳

I wake from my nap, and Coyote returns to sit next to me on the fallen tree.

I ask, "What were you doing kneeling at the base of that waterfall?"

Coyote responds, "Praying. Thanking the Creator. Soaking up His creation and using the boundless energy I receive from the waterfall and trees and specks of sunlight for the highest good. Sending it to a loved one, a stranger, my own heart, or simply back to the forest to keep beauty circulating round and round. This is the path of never-ending love, and it is our responsibility to help maintain the path."

I say, "I want to learn how to pray like you. Will you teach me?"

Coyote responds, "You already know how, which is why I am here. You began learning back in the womb and perhaps long before. Everyone can speak with God, just as everyone can heal and everyone can love and the funny thing is that everyone is searching for the secret, but you cannot find the secret because it lives deep in your heart. The place beyond the pines. The horizon where the sky meets the sea. The simple breath before responding. The land of touch. Taste. Missed chances and pits in your stomach and relief in your fingertips as they pass through her hair.

It's the turn of the key when you don't know what lies beyond the door. Not the hand that turns or the key itself or even the door, but the surrender. The stillness. The mysterious pull towards the unknown. That's the heart. That's where truth lives. And that's a deep prayer."

I say, "Wow. Beautiful. I've never met someone so mystical yet grounded at the same time. How do you remain balanced?"

Coyote replies, "This is an important question. Many of the early followers of Christ were mystics, which means they encountered God directly. I learned from Meister Eckhart, the Desert Elders, Teresa of Ávila, and of course, the Prophets. I learned from them to remain grounded through the name of Christ. I know who I am encountering, and I know He is trustworthy. This foundation provides immense freedom to explore the depths within and without."

I say, "Fascinating. I have been searching for a way that merges nature-based spirituality with

Christ's true teachings. A way that feels both freeing and grounded. I've never heard of Christian Mysticism, yet it feels familiar. What is your opinion of visions and other spiritual gifts?"

Coyote responds, "Spiritual gifts may arise by the grace of God, but do not seek them, and do not cling to them."

✳✳✳

I say, "My ankles are itching. I think I got poison ivy when we walked off the trail. Tell me, if a perfect God created all this, why would he create things like poison ivy?"

Coyote smirks, "I wonder what wisdom your discomfort is trying to teach you. Remember, nature is not perfect in the lonely way we see perfection. Sometimes the hummingbird goes into a sugar coma, sometimes the deer is eaten by wolves, and sometimes you get poison ivy.

But God makes no mistakes.

Nature is a reflection of the Creator's perfect character, but we are blinded by how we think creation ought to look. We see flaws and discomfort where God sees beauty and lessons."

I say, "I'm not sure what lesson there is to learn here."

Coyote replies, "Open your eyes, and your itchy ankles will direct you to a path you would never take when perfectly comfortable."

✳ ✳ ✳

I notice Coyote's sandals. They look old. The soles are so thin I doubt they provide any comfort whatsoever. I bet he can feel every little rock and thorn in the path.

I ask, "How do you maintain a positive attitude after hiking all this time in broken sandals?"

Coyote responds, "I am blessed with ease and force. I am blessed with faith and uncertainty. I am blessed with answers and questions. I am blessed with sleep and wide-eyed nights. I am blessed with a curious mind and a forgiving heart. I am blessed with an aging body and an eternal soul. I am blessed with thriving rivers and fallen trees. I am blessed with steady hands and restless feet.

I am blessed for countless reasons that I am not aware of and countless more to come.

All thanks to the Author of Life."

✳✳✳

We stop to rest along the riverbank. A heaviness comes over me, and I say, "I want to forget about certain painful experiences, so I can move on. Is this possible?"

Coyote places his right hand on my left shoulder, and says, "Look at the river. Water holds memory. This memory never vanishes, only transitions into a new form. And when two or more jump into a living river, it's a gathering of remembrance that cannot be put into words. The slippery, unspeakable language called surrender."

"I don't understand," I say.

Coyote continues, "The way is through, my friend. And I will go with you. But first, let us take a dip."

Coyote removes his knapsack and worn-out sandals and, without a second thought, dives into the river. I panic, worrying it's too shallow. That he'll hit his head. That he won't come back to the surface. But sure enough, his gray-haired grinning head pops out of the water like a breaching dolphin.

Coyote slowly swims to a pool closer to the bank with water that appears unmoving, but with a closer look, I see that the water is slowly spiraling. He reaches the pool and gets on his back with arms spread out and palms facing up, still as a leaf on a river and floating just the same. I always wondered how people float on water. It doesn't make sense.

I remove my heavy backpack, untie my leather boots, and slowly walk into the river. It's much colder than I expected, but after the initial shock, quite refreshing.

I swim over to Coyote and try this whole floating thing for myself. I get on my back with arms stretched out, brace myself, hold my breath, slightly paddle to stay afloat like a helicopter, and I sink.

I try again, and once more, sink after a few seconds. This goes on for some time. At least a dozen attempts. I'm getting frustrated, especially after glancing over at Coyote, calm as can be with a soft grin, looking up at the sky and floating on top of the water.

I decide to try one more time, but I'm too exhausted to keep paddling, so I simply let go with my arms stretched out and see what happens, figuring it wouldn't be the worst thing to sink at this point. But I don't sink. I float! I let out a sigh with a grin much like Coyote's, and I notice the treetops swaying with the breeze. I weigh the same, but feel lighter. It doesn't make sense.

After floating in silence, a heaviness wells up inside of me, but I quickly stop the tears. I almost sink again, and then notice my heartbeat causing ripples in the pool and meeting the ripples from Coyote, crashing into each other to then disappear into the whole river. I honestly can't tell if this is really happening, but it feels comforting.

Coyote looks my way with a nod of the head, and we silently float there for many minutes, maybe hours, watching the slowly rotating canopy of trees, as if we are watching the earth spin to its own heartbeat.

***

I say, "Before we swam in the river, I felt like a prisoner in my own mind. Now I feel more at peace. Plus, my ankles are no longer itchy! What happened?"

Coyote responds, "It's not the river that heals. It's the relationship. The trust. When you loosen your grip on life enough to let God catch you."

I say, "What does it look like to let God catch me in everyday life?"

Coyote replies, "It's following the gentle invitation to the river to pray and weep and float.

It's sitting with your back against the big oak and allowing acorns to fall from the heavens, trusting that they won't knock you out, and even if they do, trusting that here with this oak tree is exactly where you need to be. There is healing in simply bringing yourself to the point on God's map that makes Him jump up and down, which may be why those acorns began falling in the first place!

It's that split moment between hearing the thunder and seeing your niece's wide eyes and bouncing up to grab her hand, turning the storm into a baptism of awe.

Do you see? It's the relationship that heals. The invisible piece to any puzzle. The meeting point. The open invitation to depth. The living combined expression of you, the river, the tree, and anyone you find yourself in relationship with, coming together at this curiously perfect time."

✳✳✳

We wake to a new day. I face the rising sun and say a prayer that's more like a plea, "Christ, if you are real, give me a sign. Show me a bald eagle before the day is over. But not just any bald eagle—the biggest I've ever seen."

Coyote and I cover three miles along the river, passing dozens of sycamore trees with white bark that shimmers in the sun. We see many hawks, but no bald eagle.

We cover three more miles on a faint path through meadows of budding lupine, and I see a big bird flying the opposite direction. Coyote points, and as I look closely, I see its bald head. But I've seen bigger.

We continue on the trail, and I notice a big, brown feather on the ground. I ask, "Do you know what kind of bird this belongs to?"

Coyote replies, "No, I've never seen a feather like this. The sun will set soon, so let's camp here for the night."

Well, that settles it. No massive bald eagle. No sign from Christ. I look to the west with the sun escaping over the golden horizon and notice a peculiar mountaintop in the distance. Most of the mountain is covered in green trees, but the summit is bare rock.

I ask, "What's the name of that mountain?"

Coyote replies, "It goes by many names. The locals call it Resh Nesher."

I ask, "What does that mean?"

Coyote replies, "Eagle Head."

I whisper to myself, "That wasn't supposed to happen."

THE RUINS

We made it through the valley. That was a tough section of the trail. Although, now that we're through, my backpack feels lighter. I wonder if Coyote secretly put some of my supplies in his knapsack to lighten my load.

He is different than I expected. He truly embodies peace. I see now that I misjudged him. I have met people who are deeply connected with nature, and people who are deeply dedicated to Christ, but never someone who integrates the two. That is, until meeting Coyote. He is both wise and childlike. I could learn a great deal from him.

Ultimately, it's not his words that impact me most, but his actions. He walks with such presence and speaks with such heart. I probably would have turned back if it wasn't for him.

✱✱✱

We arrive at a plateau with traces of a village. It feels important here.

I ask, "Why does God allow some civilizations to flourish and others to fall?"

Coyote points to a bed of flowering mugwort, and says, "Why don't you ask this butterfly?"

I see its broken wing with such a rich shade of blue that it blends in with the equally blue sky. Before I could even consider asking a question, the butterfly says without words, "We sign a sacred pact with our Creator while in the cocoon, promising to never harm the ecosystem. This may look like taking more than we need from a flower or ignoring the blessing of nectar. And when we cause harm, the scales must be rebalanced. The wrongs must be made right.

This is when the Creator gently invites us to change. If we do not accept this invitation, He orchestrates challenging situations to heal the wounded edges of our wings so we can once again fly towards Him. There is no other way to maintain an existence where anything is possible. And this is not a war between us and the flowers, but a battle between us and ourselves, between the light and dark within."

I interrupt, "What about when we have done nothing to deserve suffering?"

The butterfly responds, "This wisdom is for the Creator alone, not for me, not for you, not even for the eagle at her highest point. There is only One with the all-seeing perspective required to maintain universal balance."

The butterfly gracefully flies closer, lands on my shoulder, and says, "Tell me, whose fault is it when a flower wilts? The sun? The rain? The wounded butterfly? The dried-up flower itself?"

I say, "I think it depends on the situation."

The butterfly flutters its wings, and says, "If you see the relationship between us and the flowers as a war, then you will see everything as an attack. The war has already been won, but you decide how to navigate your battles.

Consider the possibility that the Creator knows what He is doing, even when you are in pain, even when the world is on fire, even when it seems as if the scales are not tipping in your favor."

***

I look to Coyote, and ask, "Do you think the Garden of Eden was real?"

He responds, "We are close to the Eternal Garden when we are close to God's image. When we do good simply because that's what feels right. Not to follow the rules, not to obey a book, not to purify our karma, not even to get to heaven. Doing good without a reason brings us back to the Garden. And when we are in right relationship with God, this goodness naturally pours out of us like rivers of living water."

I ask, "What does this goodness look like?"

Coyote responds, "Tell me, where do you feel most alive?"

I say, "Well, in the woods. When I'm with someone I love. When doing a hard thing."

Coyote responds, "And how do you naturally want to show up in those moments?"

I say, "With love. Joy. Peace. Patience. Kindness. Faithfulness. Gentleness. Self-control."

Coyote smiles, "Those are the characteristics of God. When we live into these qualities, we align with our original image. We return to the Garden."

✳✳✳

I pick up a dried corn husk with seeds inside, and ask, "What if my heart messes up God's plan?"

Coyote responds, "Impossible. There is nothing any seen or unseen being can do to stop the Creator from harvesting His garden.

Sure, the heart can lead us astray. But the heart is also what allows us to connect intimately with the Creator, beyond the words on a page, so suppressing the heart is not the way."

I ask, "How do I guard my heart from evil?"

Coyote responds, "Tell me, how does a garden flourish?"

I say, "Well, it needs sun, rain, and good soil. Oh, and the gardener must fight off weeds and critters."

Coyote responds, "Yes, the plants need a nourishing environment, but you cannot avoid the critters that eat your garden. You can, however, cultivate soil so rich that these bites are not a battle but a purification, pruning the unclean edges of your leaves.

Raccoons are most attracted to gardens with lots of fruit. Lots of life. And this is how it is in the spiritual realm. Cultivate faith, hope, and love in your heart, and the deceiver will feel threatened by your fruits of the spirit.

But do not be afraid, for you are untouchable in the Kingdom of God.

If you fear without grabbing hold of the Creator's hand, you throw the deceiver a couple berries here, a couple carrots there, and in a moment of pride, you may throw him the key to walk right into your garden.

The master gardener knows better.

He does not focus his energy on fighting what he perceives as evil. Instead, he tends the soil, honors the sun, and thanks the rain.

His work is his worship."

I respond, "I see. So, spiritual protection naturally comes when communing with God in my daily life?"

Coyote smiles, "Indeed. First, invite Him in, then cultivate a heart that makes Him feel at home."

***

I ask, "What does the world need right now?"

Coyote responds, "There is no need to save the world from anything. Simply deepen your circle. Deepen your relationships with others, with yourself, and most importantly, with God. Learn to listen and respond with awareness. Make amends where necessary. Forgive, repent, forgive, repent. Start with whatever you are avoiding."

I say, "I hear you. I am struggling to forgive those who wronged me. I'm not sure they deserve my forgiveness."

Coyote glances at my backpack, which I realize is leaking water. In fact, my back is damp. I open my pack and see a crack in my canteen. Then it dawns on me. I have been so focused on how others hurt me that I couldn't see the slippery trail I've left behind me.

Coyote nods, and says, "We can refill at the Living Spring. But know this—if you harbor resentment in your heart, the water will quench the body, but not the soul."

I look down, ashamed, and say, "Please teach me to forgive. I have tried for years because I'm told it's in my best interest to forgive, but the anger keeps resurfacing. There has to be another way."

Coyote responds, "True forgiveness cannot be forced. It naturally comes when we allow our messy humanity to connect us in a more compassionate way with the humanity in others. We do not love through perfection. Only through the cracks. And none of us are innocent, so we all need God's gift of grace. Hear this, and you are on your way."

I say, "What if I don't want certain people back into my life?"

Coyote responds, "We are called to love everyone, but that does not mean trusting everyone."

I look out into the distance and reflect on Coyote's words. I see a river to the left that might have clean water to refill my canteen, then a pond to the right with stagnant water not fit for drinking. One is good for swimming and the other is good for fishing. I see that the pond is prone to developing algae and the river is prone to flooding nearby trees. Each has its struggles. Each is beautiful in its own way.

And I finally understand.

I say, "Part of me wants to be in the world with others, while another part wants to stay in the wilderness by myself. You seem to be doing great out here on your own, right?"

Coyote responds, "Careful with your words. We all need a way to share our story. To give love. To be loved. To know that our suffering is worthy of holding.

There is an end in sight for the lone wolf, but for the pack of two or more, nothing ends. Nothing can break the bond of unconditional love, as this seeps into the very fabric of existence.

God is the weaver, but you choose the color. The thickness. The feel of the yarn as you pass through the needle of birth and death, death and birth, holding each end as sacred as the one before.

Yeshua had his disciples. The bees have their buzzing hive. And there is a community needing you as much as you need them."

✳✳✳

I notice bird droppings on Coyote's shoulder, and ask, "Why does God allow bad things to happen to good people?"

Coyote responds, "Because God's priority is preparing the soul, not comforting the human mind or body."

I ask, "What does that mean?"

Coyote responds, "Tell me, how is an arrow made?"

I say, "Well, a piece of tree is carved down. And a piece of flint is shaped into a point."

Coyote responds, "Yes. The tree undergoes great transformation, and so does the flint. Selecting, chopping, carving, heating, bending, testing, and finally, blessing.

Some steps are clearly on purpose and others are seemingly on accident. But all steps are necessary so the tree and flint can become the arrow that hits the mark."

***

I ask, "What about all the people who have killed in the name of God?"

Coyote quietly pulls a bow and arrow from his knapsack. I don't even know how it fit in there. Then I hear leaves rustling behind us.

I turn around to a mountain lion leaping towards us out of nowhere, and at the last possible second, Coyote shoots an arrow piercing the mountain lion's exposed chest.

The big cat falls to the ground.

It all happened so fast. I feel my heart pounding faster and faster. Thank God Coyote was prepared.

He walks over to the mountain lion taking its final breath, performs the sign of the cross over his chest, and prays, "Creator, thank you for this abundance. I honor this animal for its bravery and thank it for its life. May we make good use of the nourishment this animal provides. In Christ's name, Amen."

I open my eyes and see tears falling from Coyote's face, then he turns to me and says, "God created the trees and flint, but it is our choice how we use the arrow."

In this moment, I wonder if my running away from religion has been less about God and more about people.

It's true, I have been harmed by those who claim to be followers of Christ, but I have also been harmed by those who do not. Maybe they were all misusing their free will. Maybe one misled Christian doesn't make Christ's teachings any less divine. Maybe God really is good.

Now that I think about it, I would rather follow a God who doesn't force me to follow Him, but allows me to choose.

****

I say, "If heaven is real, do you think we get there by faith or by good deeds?"

Coyote responds, "Two things can be true at the same time. There is a bridge between knowing and feeling. Between eternity and a moment. This bridge does not resemble any we have walked before, because this is a bridge of three. The mind, body, and spirit. The Father, Son, and Holy Spirit. A bridge found out there and within, often wherever you are not looking. Above your head, behind the mirror, some distant moment when your past and future and present are aligned.

You cannot build the bridge with white-knuckled effort. Grace is gifted to you whether you know it or not, and it is your decision to accept or decline this eternal offering. You cannot take or steal it. It is a gift or nothing at all.

If you choose to receive the gift, then the bridge appears, and the evidence of your belief lies in your desire to clear the bridge of debris, so you may continue walking towards the divine."

✳✳✳

I ask, "How will I know when I am ready for true love?"

Coyote responds, "I will share a story. There was a man who uncovered something about himself he didn't like, so he covered it back up, piled the dirt even higher.

Eventually, God sent the rain and exposed that wounded part of himself, and so the man covered it up again for no one to see, with even more dirt this time.

Then God brought a wildfire in the form of a careless teenager striking a match during a drought, and then there were no more trees to surround the obvious mound of dirt. So the man built a clever wall of thorns around his secret for no one to enter, especially himself.

And finally, God sent her, the one to bring him to his knees, who was searching for a place to bury her own wounded secrets. She finds his makeshift wall of thorns that he built to blend in with nature and not be known by others, and she thinks this is a good place to hide her secrets. As she digs and tosses her shame into the dark hole, she hits his old rotting treasure, and both darknesses break into tiny pieces of what appears to be gold at the center.

A stiff pain of disbelief in his right ankle and a sharp pain of sadness in her left ear brings a clear choice—continue covering up the treasure with dirt and shame and go their separate ways once they crumble the bridge between them beyond repair, or consider the possibility that this is not fool's gold. Consider the possibility that this meeting of two broken people is a precious gift from above, orchestrated to bring them to their knees at this precise moment, when their hearts were cracked open enough to trust in God to guide them home."

✳✳✳

I ask, "How can I prepare to be a good parent?"

Coyote responds, "Prepare right now, by cultivating your relationship with the divine. When your relationship with the Creator grows, your ability to be a good parent naturally grows.

Sure, it is possible to build the skills of fatherhood by learning to communicate with your spouse, learning to discipline lovingly and directly, and of course, relearning how to have fun. But if you learn these things without first going through God, these will be like skills on a resume instead of qualities etched into your heart. You may speak to your children impeccably, but if those words are not coming from a divine love in your heart, the words will fall flat, and your children will feel it.

So put your relationship with God first. And be sure your spouse does the same. But do not tell your children exactly how God looks to you. Leave some mystery. Let their imagination run wild and fill in what your blind spots are missing.

Your job is to love your family the way God loves you. To show your children what it looks like to be a devoted father, a devoted husband, a devoted son of God in this complicated world.

Beyond this, your job is to get out of God's way. Allow Him to raise your children while you provide a stable foundation for them to grow their own way in this world."

✳✳✳

I say, "I don't like most churches. They feel suffocating. How do you know your religion is the way?"

Coyote responds, "You have been hurt. The pain in your heart is real. And it is true, there are plenty of imperfections with the current state of religion. This is our fault, not God's fault. You say churches feel constricting to you. Some have felt that way to me too. Instead of discussing religion, let us discuss Christ, who you seem to be curious about."

I say, "Okay, so how do you know Christ is the way to God?"

Coyote shouts, "Now that's a good question! I could share some theological reasons, but they don't matter. We are speaking about the heart, after all. That's the funny thing about faith. The mind must decrease so the heart may increase.

Now, as for your question, what I know to be true is that when I lost everything, Christ met me there. When I couldn't see a way through to the next season, the next day, even the next minute, Christ carried me through. No judgment. No demanding of praise. No reminding me of all the ways

I cursed him. He simply held me. I wouldn't be here without Him."

I say, "I am glad you found Christ. Or rather, that you found each other. It must feel comforting to be so sure of your path. I hope to find that level of clarity one day."

Coyote responds, "Tell me, how do you know you'd like to spend your life with someone?"

I ask, "Like marriage?"

Coyote responds, "Yes, like marriage."

I say, "Well, I guess we go on dates and see what happens."

Coyote continues, "Precisely. You spend quality time together to learn who she really is. You see if the two of you are good for each other and good for the world. This is how it is with your heavenly partner."

I respond, "I'll be honest, I am becoming more and more curious about Christ, but I don't know who he is to me. I would like to know the real, unfiltered Christ, not who the world says he is. But it's not like I can sit down with him."

Coyote responds, "Why not?"

I laugh, "Well...how?"

Coyote responds, "If you'd like, I will guide you."

I notice the peace in Coyote's eyes. He really does seem trustworthy. "Okay," I say. "Let's sit with Christ."

Coyote nods, then removes his shoes. I do the same, and feel the cold, rough dirt under my feet. We simultaneously sit in a cross-legged position.

Coyote draws what seems like a primitive fish in the dirt, then says, "Let's begin with three, deep breaths. In through your nose, and out through your mouth. Feel the holy ground beneath you as you breath. Now, close your eyes. Imagine you are in a safe place. Any place that comes to mind. Notice what you see, smell, hear, and feel. Really tune in. Notice where the shadows fall and where they don't fall. Now, imagine Christ asks to join you. Do you invite Him in?"

I nod, and Coyote continues, "How does He appear? What do you notice about Him? No need to be perfect in His presence. He wants you to be authentic. What would you like to ask Him? What would you like to tell Him? Let's remain here for some time, in silence. And if you are struggling to engage any of your senses in this place, ask Christ for help."

I sink into the meditation, and after what seems

like only a few seconds, I hear Coyote say, "Okay, when you're ready, gently come back."

I open my eyes, and the light of the sun is shining brighter than before, and yet, the sun does not compare to the light I witnessed in that meditation.

I say, "I have never experienced something like that. I saw myself floating in the middle of the ocean, much like you and I floated on that river. Christ appeared directly above me, floating in the air. In his face, I saw complete passion and peace. Utter power and gentleness. Then I realized he was not only in front of me, but also supporting me in the ocean itself, and encouraging me in the call of the seagulls, and guiding me in the whispers of the breeze. I felt held from all directions. Now that I think about it, floating in the middle of the ocean sounds scary, but I wasn't afraid. I was at peace."

Coyote nods, "It sounds like you met the real Christ. Remember, you can always return to that place."

I say, "I need to sit with this. I don't know what this means to me."

Coyote responds, "Take your time. No need to have it all figured out."

✳✳✳

I ask, "Do you think miracles still happen, like the days of Yeshua?"

Coyote responds, "We are not Yeshua, but we can all perform miracles. When someone is suffering, heavy, unsure if they are worthy of a better life, this is fertile soil for a miracle to sprout. It is the lost who allow for miracles. Their willingness to surrender and believe and receive the gift of change.

All you need to do is see the good in them. See that they are worthy of love. And then offer them that love. A 30-second hug can do it. A genuine look in their eyes can do it.

Combine these loving acts with an unwavering belief that God can heal them if you simply get out of His way, then a miracle is bound to happen."

THE CAVE

We made it through the ruins. Coyote's morning tea over the campfire is extra tasty lately. I wonder if he's doing something different when preparing it.

Anyway, I began hiking up this mountain with questions I needed answered, and now I have even more questions. I see now that my belief in everything was really a belief in nothing. I used to think every god was true, and maybe I still do, but I'm beginning to see Christ everywhere. It's interesting and unexpected. I don't know what it means.

I've been seeking for so long that it feels foreign to be found, even momentarily. I thought I was free all those years, but maybe I was just afraid to commit to a path. Maybe I was a slave to my fear.

But no more. From now on, I will do my best to believe from a true place, not reacting from those who hurt me.

✻✻✻

After walking several miles in silence, a sudden flash of despair comes over me, and I say, "Coyote, I'm dizzy. Maybe from the altitude. I need to take a break."

Coyote responds, "Good idea. Let's sit on this log for a while and then take refuge in that cave over there."

I say, "Okay. I don't have the energy for a question right now. I just need your help."

Some birds sing in the distance, and Coyote says, "A cry for help is the purest question there is, my friend. I will sit with you as long as you need."

"Thank you," I say.

Coyote nods and says, "Now, listen to those birds. The lighthearted songs from sparrows are encouraging, but it's the heavy songs from mourning doves that truly strike a chord. If you can hear them singing, the battle is already won."

I take a moment and listen to the birds. I close my eyes, try to slow my breathing, and after some time, I hear something. First, the quick and bright chirps. Then, underneath, the low and slow coos. Once I notice the cooing, the chirping gets even brighter. It's almost as if one is incomplete without the other, creating a symphony together.

I let out a heavy sigh of relief, not from lack of discomfort, but for a moment, somehow, I know everything will be okay. I sense an abundance of love all around me, starting with Coyote and extending throughout the mountain.

Then the sharp pain in my temples begins to fade, and I can see more clearly.

✱✱✱

I say, "This has happened to me before. The dizziness. When I'm close to a breakthrough. Closer to my purpose. That's when I feel most vulnerable. Why is this?"

Coyote responds, "You are moving through an important transformation. Obstacles are a good sign. Obstacles mean you are walking the path you are called to walk, because the false forces are threatened by the holy direction you're taking. Be wary of the comfortable path, and be patient with yourself."

Coyote hands me a jagged rock, and says, "Feel this rock in your hand. The edges need not be rounded. No need for it to be easy to hold, but let it become natural."

I look at the rock in my hand. The edges are dangerously sharp, so I hold my breath to remain still and avoid cutting myself. But I can't keep this up, so I get back to my breath, deeper and deeper, slower and slower.

I wonder what's on the other side of the rock, so I flip it over, and I'm shocked.

I look at Coyote, and he says, "This is good. The feeling is not familiar at life's surface but calls on a deeper part of you. The soul is not easily held. A true path is not easily known. But it is here, elated by each breath you take from the surface to reach further into your own depths."

I nod, and Coyote continues, "You can hold your breath in the palm of your hands longer than you know. You can know yourself deeper than you think is possible.

Allow yourself to be surprised by what you uncover. Allow God to hold you just as you hold this rock in your hand. And when you lean on Him, you may become dizzy, but you will not faint."

✳ ✳ ✳

We enter the cave, light a fire, and I ask, "What if I can't handle the life I am called to live?"

Coyote responds, "If it is fire that will cleanse you, then you will welcome the flames. If it is water that will cleanse you, then you will welcome the rain.

And rest assured, God will never place a holy battle in your path without also placing a holy sword at your feet.

That is His way.

He is the master of balancing a great challenge with greater support to pull you through and uncover your unique gifts along the way.

When you hold His eternal open hand and walk through the flames instead of avoiding them, the whole of existence benefits from your brave steps."

✳✳✳

I wrestle with my pen and notebook, and ask, "What is the language of the heart?"

Coyote responds, "Presence. Unadulterated experiencing. You cannot put what the heart speaks into words. You cannot capture it. You cannot understand it with the mind.

The language of the heart is inescapable yet fleeting. It is the words naturally unraveling before you can think of the words. It is the tears falling from unattached openness. It is Yeshua going to the desert to pray, opening to His Father. It is this work of praying in the wilderness before and after performing miracles, time and time again, setting an example, building a bridge for us to walk into His sacred here and now heart.

In moments of heartfelt stillness, your true image as a reflection of God is more clear. This is what is meant by eternity.

He is here.

He is within you.

He is open to connection.

But this will always be an invitation. There is no barging through the door. This is a relationship with a gentle open hand, a reaching out when ready, and a third spirit connecting you two that lives in the holy water at the entrance and makes the tip of the crown shine."

* * *

I say, "I am now seeing glimpses of God's hand at work, but then He vanishes. I still feel a wall between us. How do I break through?"

Coyote responds, "God is never far. You are not distant like a tree and a star, but close like a leaf and a tree, a planet revolving around a star, a universe staring back at you from your lover's eye. The threads are there for those who care to touch them, and remember, these threads are never completely severed, no matter how disconnected you become.

God is never far. Not even death can separate you from the divine, not even pain, not even your false self. Lie and cheat your way through life, and eventually your soul will speak louder than your pride, and you will be on the path of oneness again."

I ask, "What is this path of oneness?"

Coyote responds, "We may take different routes, but we all attempt the same journey, the journey of reuniting with our Creator. It is a blessing that you are now taking this journey consciously.

And I assure you, if it is truth you're after, then you will find it, and you will see that you don't need to look far."

I ask, "Where do you recommend looking?"

Coyote smiles, "Busy people are difficult for God to reach. Slow down, and there He is. Create, and there He is. What better way to reunite with our Creator than to create?"

*** * ***

I say, "I hear people say that we are all connected, and I want it to be true, but what does that actually mean?"

Coyote points, "Look at the hummingbird over there on the branch. Really look at her with your heart cracked open to all her beauty. Do you see her?"

I respond, "Yes, I see her."

Coyote continues, "Now, tell her how special she is. Really feel the words as you release them in her direction."

I take a breath and notice the hummingbird's blue wing feathers, then her green chest feathers. Her chest almost looks metallic, with the sun now reflecting off the bright green. I say out loud, "Wow, you really are beautiful."

Coyote says, "At this very moment, you are expanding the hummingbird's heart through simple adoration. And then she transforms the nearby poppy flower into a new shade of red through the loving hum of her wings. And then the poppy flower transforms the child in you through a red the child has never seen before, even if he is colorblind, because we are dealing with something beyond the usual senses.

And this is how the holy threads reconnect. This is the unceasing prayer Saint Paul spoke about two thousand years ago. This is how reuniting with God is playing out before our eyes, all from simple, open-hearted presence."

✳ ✳ ✳

I ask, "How can I distinguish between the voice of Light and the voice of darkness?"

Coyote responds, "Look at the fireflies. The Light gently nudges you to appreciate creation, while the dark urges you to capture those fireflies before it's too late.

Look at the scrape on your knee. The Light encourages you for taking a leap, while the dark scares you into thinking you're on the wrong path.

Look at the fire. The Light invites you to burn off your harmful patterns, while the dark tempts you to use the fire to become more powerful than your neighbor.

Look at the river we crossed. The Light guides you toward the challenging path that you can handle together, while the dark brings paralyzing doubt that nearly leads you to turn around.

Look at your mistakes that harmed others. The Light calls you into a change of heart, while the dark says, 'It doesn't matter, as long as you are happy.'

Look at your accomplishments. The Light invites you to share abundance with those in need, while the dark tries to convince you to praise your-self.

Look at the valleys when you didn't know if you would make it through. The Light proves trustworthy by giving you strength, often how you least expect, while the dark tells you that the Light has abandoned you, and then tempts you with momentary relief that only covers up the pain.

Do you see? The Light sows seeds of truth, love, and repentance, while the dark sows seeds of doubt, fear, and pride.

One is true Light guiding us through darkness, and one is darkness pretending to be light.

Each moment is an opportunity to welcome one or the other inside of you."

✳ ✳ ✳

I burn myself on the fire and shout, "Ouch! I really can't catch a break. How will I hear God's voice if I can't hear my own body before it's too late?"

Coyote looks at me like you do when a child asks why the sky is blue. As if he asked this very question at my age.

And he responds, "I sense you are drawn to the drastically moving corners of this world. The adventures, the seeking, the tall grass blowing in the wind. And I want you to know, it is all moving. Even the seemingly unwavering pieces of this world. The mountain, the rock, the grandfather tree, this planet, your own beating heart. It's all moving. It's all changing. But the drastic changes are all you will see and all you will seek if you don't become still enough to appreciate the subtleties."

Coyote hands back the rock that I set down, and says, "Hold this rock until your arms tremble more from the weight of connection than from the weight of the rock.

Then, you will begin to hear God's whispers before the shouts. Then, you will recognize His still, small voice."

✳✳✳

I say, "I have read many spiritual and religious books, and although I learned from them, I do not feel closer to God. What am I doing wrong?"

Coyote responds, "Imagine you are on a porch reading a scientific book about fireflies, and then you look up to see countless fireflies magically appearing and disappearing as they do summer evenings in this stretch of country. Do you keep reading or do you witness the real thing?"

I respond, "I would watch the actual fireflies in front of me."

"Of course," he says. "And this is how it is with our Creator. Even the most brilliant words will not capture His depth, His essence. He is to be experienced. He is to be communed with. He is to be felt through your very eyes and ears and trembling hands.

This is what God desires from you. To be together, in the pleasant moments and the painful moments. To receive your spontaneous prayers. To interact through His creation. The fireflies, the moon, the spouse far on the other side of the bed. Let the questions about good and evil and what happens after death come if they need to, but remember to be with your Creator, through His creation."

I respond, "But how do I get out of my mind enough to commune with creation in this way?"

Coyote responds, "Through awe. It takes the heart of a child to choose the moment over the intellect. And when you do, it is this childlike presence that opens you up to receive the wisdom of the Word."

Coyote and I simultaneously look outside the cave and into the dark forest, and what do you know, countless fireflies are bouncing around like the glow-in-the-dark stars on my childhood bedroom ceiling.

We glance at each other, let out two howling laughs that sound more like one, and enjoy this moment together.

✳✳✳

I say, "I am all out of questions for tonight. I think I overreacted with the fire. I'm grateful to be here with you, burns and all."

We notice a yellow bird fly across the entrance of the cave, and Coyote says with a smile, "One of the oldest gifts is two open hearts in action.

It is a thousand yellow roses thrown into the air and never landing.

It is the third spark of fire thanking the first and second.

It is the potter and the clay and the sipper of tea, all honoring each other in their own way.

It is no longer a student and teacher, but it is now the trees and the reflection of trees on the river."

Coyote and I both nod, like when we first met on the trail, and we lie down on opposite sides of the fire to sleep.

✳✳✳

We wake up, still warm from the fire, and I ask, "How did you keep the fire burning while we slept?"

Coyote responds, "When a fire is stoked long enough, and the coals reach a deep enough red, and the prayers spoken while collecting the wood are true enough, then I can rest as long as I need, and the fire still lives when I wake."

I say, "Fascinating. How does that work?"

Coyote responds, "The fire has become internal. It is no longer only the elements out there. It is the outside and inside working together. It is human and divine working together. It is the physical and spirit together as one. It is the complete cycle.

The Great Fire is always burning at earth's core. It started long ago, sparked from a flame on the other side of God's thumb. Nothing comes from nothing. Everything is born from something, so the pieces we know as life have come at a cost. Our existence means something else cannot exist, so it is our duty to live up to the role. The role of being chosen to live. We are all worthy, and we are all here for a reason."

Coyote and I look into the flames, and he continues, "Remember, when playing with fire, give all the glory to the original fire tender, as it was in the beginning, as it is now, and so it will be in a world without end."

✳✳✳

We begin packing to leave, and I say, "I am tempted to stay in this cave. I'm starting to feel closer with God, and I'd rather be here with Him than with those I don't trust."

Coyote looks into my eyes with great care, reminding me of my childhood imaginary friend, then asks, "What are you running from?"

I let out a deep sigh, and say, "I don't know."

Coyote responds, "Even if you stayed in this cave for months or years or the remainder of this life, humanity would still be etched into your bones. Your ancestors still guiding you. Every word spoken or unspoken still part of your story.

We need one another, and this is not something to run from. This is something to celebrate. The fabric of humanity runs through your bones, so why not go with it and direct the red thread toward never-ending destinations that heal and invite countless others into the sacred tapestry.

The real master is willing and able to meet God wherever he is. At the post office. While driving in rush hour. During the beginning, middle, and resolution of a conflict. The real master serves a higher purpose in the mundane. In relationships. This is why we're here, after all. No one heals in isolation. It's a communal effort whether you're aware of it or not."

Coyote puts his right hand on my left shoulder, and continues, "My dear friend, whatever you are doing, let it bring you closer to humanity, not further away. Whether on a solitary pilgrimage or in a busy city. Let your practices open you up to the gift of connection, just as you have opened up to me."

I feel something bubbling up within me. Coyote's words have fascinated me since meeting him, but this is different.

I lower my head, and say, "Coyote, I think I have been running away from many things. Betrayal. Failure. The fear of not being enough. Afraid to commit to a path, a community, a place, a God."

Tears escape my eyes for the first time in years, then Coyote gently squeezes my shoulder, and this releases the flood. From head to heart, from sob to deeper sob. I sense the now free current within me taking a turn to the dry banks of grief, then to the overgrown land of fear, then to the seemingly barren land of trust, and now there's only one thing left to do—arrive barefoot and broken with an offering of faith.

I collapse to my knees, and land softly on the dirt. I pray, and the One I pray to becomes more familiar with each honest word. I weep, and the questions fade away with each tear.

I cry out, "Christ, I need you. I don't know where I am going, but I want to go with you. I don't fully know who you are, but I have witnessed your goodness. I can't keep going alone. Show me the way."

I look up at the fire's shadow on the cave wall and see a scroll unraveling with the secrets I have been seeking. A voice like rushing water tells me not to write it down, but to place it in my heart. I do this, and the scroll vanishes, along with my fear.

My crying slows to a relieving deep calm, like the first breath after a fever breaks.

I feel at peace. Much like floating on the river. Much like visiting Christ in the meditation. But this peace is...different.

Coyote removes his hand from my shoulder, nods, and I look down, surprised to see my hand rubbing my chest.

A NEW BEGINNING

Coyote and I finish packing up, and silently watch the sun peek over the horizon, in between the trees. I thank God for this cave's shelter, and Coyote does the same. I feel compelled to pour my water onto the fire, trusting that God will provide. And then we continue up the mountain.

I feel lighter today, as if I left something in the cave I no longer needed, not just the water. Come to think of it, the air feels more familiar with each step, with a scent I haven't smelled since childhood. Minty, piney, fresh, a scent that somehow spans all seasons. I remember joyfully running around barefoot as a child towards nothing at all.

I pass it off as coincidence and keep walking until eventually, I forget altogether where I am heading and why I began this journey. I look up at the sunrise-soaked clouds and leap as high as I can to see if I can touch them, then laugh at myself for attempting such a thing.

It's brutally cold up here. My entire body aches from the long journey, yet I feel more alive than I have in years. I see my breath like smoke releasing from a chimney, showing me the internal fire is lit. I pick a snow-dusted mint leaf from the side of the trail and gently place it on my tongue, bringing me back to life even more from an explosion of flavor.

I thank God for His creation, and look back at the coast all those miles away, all those days away. The rainforest, the rivers, the valley, the plateau with ruins of a different time. This bird's-eye view allows me to witness the change and see that all the detours were necessary.

I nod with gratitude, and realize there are relationships back home that need tending.

After seven minutes or seven hours, I round a corner and see an unassuming cabin cradled by bent trees. I nearly missed it, as it blends in with nature. Actually, the trees surrounding the cabin are more lush and green than the rest of the landscape.

Now things are getting interesting, because I recognize this cabin. I've seen it before, somewhere. Maybe in a dream. Maybe not. Maybe in another life I was the very tree used to build this tiny home in the middle of this forest on top of this rugged yet inviting mountain.

I look back, excited to show my wandering companion the cabin, and he is nowhere to be found. This terrifies me. I shout for him again and again, but hear nothing. Where did he go? Is he okay? Have I been hallucinating this whole journey? I don't let myself think this way for too long, so I gather myself and continue walking towards the cabin.

Carefully, I tiptoe across the creaking porch that's more moss than wood at this point and reach out to knock the hardly functional door, and just before my cold knuckles hit the wood, the door opens.

I cannot believe my eyes.

A white-haired man glowing like an angel, who feels as much like me as I do myself. Rugged yet inviting, just like this mountain, he says with complete authority and complete loving presence, "Welcome, young one. I have been waiting for you."

I fall to my knees, partly from relief and partly from a feeling I cannot name. He picks me up, hugs me, and says, "Kneel only before God."

I respond with a trembling voice, "Um, okay, hello. I don't know what to say. I came all this way seeking answers from you, battling the elements within and out there. But now that I'm here, I am both embarrassed and pleased to say that I'm all out of questions. I was guided by a wise man named Coyote. He answered my questions with interesting riddles, and more importantly, showed me unconditional love."

I laugh, "Sometimes it was tough love, but it's what I needed. He brought me back to the moment. Back to humanity. Back to my heart. Tell me, are you the master the yellow bird told me about?"

He chuckles, "You are learning. All your seeking and all your questions are admirable, but you also have a life to live, right here in front of you. Presence is your calling. With loved ones. With birds. With enemies. With God. Remember, Yeshua often went to the desert to pray, but the important part is that He came back. He always came back and fully rejoined the world. And what was His priority when returning?"

I respond, "Well, people. Relationships. Healing."

"Correct," he says. "Coyote's riddles reached you because your heart was cracked open. Well done. As for your question about the master, perhaps you already met him. Perhaps I am a different kind of master. Perhaps you are too. There is deep wisdom in all of us. The trick is to remain open to learning from each one in your path. I see God's messengers did their job supporting you along the way and will continue to do so."

I say, "I understand. Although, I wish I could have properly thanked Coyote and said goodbye."

He responds, "Coyote knows your heart. He is always with you to the south and I am always with you to the north. You will see. Now, you cannot stay here forever, so let's savor our time together."

He motions for me to come in, walks to the humble kitchen, and adds three logs to the stove. He then hands me a steel pot and asks me to gather some snow. I do this and bring the cold pot back inside.

He places the pot on the stove, gently twists his long beard, and says, "You brought the water. I brought the fire. Now, what else shall we add?"

I open my hand, offering the remaining mint leaves I collected on the trail.

He smiles and adds the leaves to the pot of melting snow. Then he reaches up and grabs a bundle of mugwort hanging from the rafters, adding this to the pot.

We silently wait for the water to boil, and it's a silence that fills me up. The kitchen slowly fills with a sweet and earthy aroma.

We then bring the steeping tea to the small living room. He sits on the older rocking chair. It is perfectly worn and rocks smoothly back and forth, despite moving across uneven, holey floors. I sit on the newer rocking chair. It is clean and shiny, but does not rock as smoothly.

He brings his cup to his nose, smells the tea with a soft grin, and sips slowly. I do the same.

He then looks into my eyes with such presence and care that it warms my heart in a way not even the fire last night could.

And he says, "So, tell me, how is the tea?"

PARABLES UP THE MOUNTAIN

A SEEKER'S TRAIL

Joey Doherty

A REQUEST

If you were impacted by this book, here are some ways you can help spread the word:

- ⊕ Rate/review the book on Goodreads.com or Amazon.com.
- ⊕ Gift your copy to someone who might benefit from the book's message.
- ⊕ Share a photo of the book on social media and tag @joeydoherty.
- ⊕ Ask your favorite bookstore to stock the book.
- ⊕ Tell a loved one (or stranger) how the book impacted you.
- ⊕ Start a small group or book club to discuss Seeker's questions.

ACKNOWLEDGMENTS

Thank you to my friends and family who prayed for me while I wrote this book. Thank you to my parents, grandparents, and all those before me for lighting the way. Thank you to my beta readers, Sarah Morford, Iris Nabalo, Tyler Hudson, Ashley Dawson, Kelly Kohlberg, Dhanya Varughese, and Jeff Frazier. Thank you to my editors, Trace Murphy and Michael Martin. Thank you to Jacob Tanner for creating the cover art. Above all, thank you to the Holy Spirit for guiding me.

Soli Deo Gloria,
JGD

INDEX

GLOSSARY

Angels rejoice, Luke 15:7

Be like children to enter the Kingdom of Heaven, Matthew 18:3

Deceiver disguised as an angel of light, 2 Corinthians 11:14

Desert Elders, Christian hermits living in the deserts of Egypt, Palestine, Syria, and Arabia from the third to fifth century AD

Eternal blue sky, Translation of 'Tengri', god of nomadic peoples of Central Asia traced back to the fourth century BC

Fruits of the spirit, Galatians 5: 22-23

Meister Eckhart, German priest and mystic from the thirteenth century AD

Receive a new name, Revelation 2:17

Rivers of living water, John 7:38

Saint Paul, Author of fourteen books of the Bible

Saint Teresa of Ávila, Carmelite nun and Spanish mystic from the sixteenth century AD

Scroll with secrets, Revelation 10:4

Unceasing prayer, 1 Thessalonians 5:17

Wide and narrow path, Matthew 7: 13-14

Will not faint, Isaiah 40:31

Yeshua, Jesus' name in Aramaic

ABOUT THE AUTHOR

JOEY DOHERTY, LPCC, is a storyteller, clinical counselor, meditation instructor, and hiking guide. He has trained hundreds of helpers and guided thousands toward balancing the mind, body, and spirit. He enjoys backpacking, visiting old monasteries and ruins, and riding motorcycles. Joey currently lives halfway in Ohio and halfway on the road, barefoot whenever possible.

Instagram @joeydoherty
Email joeygdoherty@gmail.com
Website joeydoherty.com

TITLES BY JOEY DOHERTY

Parables Up the Mountain (2026)
Subtle Medicine (2021)
Student of the Moment (2020)
Color the World (2019)
Wild Compass (2018)
Remember to Harvest (2017)

www.ingramcontent.com/pod-product-compliance
Lightning Source LLC
Chambersburg PA
CBHW031146130726
47988CB00006B/2554